A Very Young Gardener

A Very Young Gardener

Written and Photographed by Jill Krementz

Dial Books for Young Readers New York

Also by Jill Krementz

THE FACE OF SOUTH VIETNAM
(with text by Dean Brelis)

SWEET PEA—A BLACK GIRL GROWING UP
IN THE RURAL SOUTH

WORDS AND THEIR MASTERS
(with text by Israel Shenker)

THE WRITER'S IMAGE

A VERY YOUNG DANCER

A VERY YOUNG RIDER

A VERY YOUNG GYMNAST

A VERY YOUNG CIRCUS FLYER

A VERY YOUNG SKATER

A VERY YOUNG SKIER

A VERY YOUNG MUSICIAN

THE FUN OF COOKING

LILY GOES TO THE PLAYGROUND

JACK GOES TO THE BEACH

TARYN GOES TO THE DENTIST

BENJY GOES TO A RESTAURANT

KATHERINE GOES TO NURSERY SCHOOL

JAMIE GOES ON AN AIRPLANE

ZACHARY GOES TO THE ZOO

HOLLY'S FARM ANIMALS

A VISIT TO WASHINGTON, D.C.

HOW IT FEELS WHEN A PARENT DIES

HOW IT FEELS TO BE ADOPTED

HOW IT FEELS WHEN PARENTS DIVORCE

HOW IT FEELS TO FIGHT FOR YOUR LIFE

Published by Dial Books for Young Readers
A Division of Penguin Books USA Inc.
375 Hudson Street
New York, New York 10014

Library of Congress Cataloging in Publication Data
Krementz, Jill.
A very young gardener/written and photographed by Jill Krementz.
p. cm.
Summary: Text and photographs feature highlights of the
gardening year as six-year-old Ashley grows flowers and vegetables
in her garden, looks at native plants in the woods, and visits
a botanical garden.
ISBN 0-8037-0874-2.—ISBN 0-8037-0875-0 (lib. bdg.)
1. Gardening—Juvenile literature. [1. Gardening.] I. Title.
SB457.K74 1991 635—dc20 90-2766 CIP AC

*This book is dedicated
to
Henry Wolf—
a brilliant photographer,
an inspiring mentor,
and
a wonderful friend*

Spring is definitely my favorite time of year. That's because I'm a gardener. My name is Ashley and I'm six.

I have two gardens—one for vegetables and one for flowers. I love all flowers, but daffodils are my favorite. We plant the bulbs in the fall and they blossom early in the spring.

I like to make little bouquets of flowers. The first one usually goes in a vase on my bedside table, but if there are lots of flowers Mommy and I put them all around the house.

Even though we grow most of our flowers from seed, it's still fun to go to the nursery. That's where we buy seedlings and plants. Geraniums are great because they bloom all summer long.

"Nursery" is the perfect name for a garden center because it's just like a nursery school in a way. There are lots of people to take special care of all the little seedlings.

I'm always on the lookout for something tasty to add to my herb garden. Daddy planted it for me outside our kitchen door.

My friend Lily loves to garden too. She's lucky to be named after a flower. If I were named after one, I'd like to be called Rose.

Spring is the season to buy packets of seeds for my vegetable garden. They all look so delicious that it's hard to choose. I usually get the basics like corn, peas, beans, carrots, lettuce, cucumbers, and sunflower seeds.

I also buy marigold seeds. The bugs don't like the way these flowers smell, so they stay away. That protects my vegetables.

Daddy and I make a special trip to the farmers' market to buy a sack of potatoes. We're looking for the potatoes with the most "eyes" because after we plant them, each eye will sprout into a new potato plant.

Daddy and I dig little trenches for the potatoes. Then we cover them gently with the loose earth. I have to be very careful not to hit the potatoes with my hoe because I don't want to knock off their eyes. Daddy keeps saying, "Nice and easy, Ashley."

We plant both red and white potatoes because we like both kinds. Potatoes are a "never-fail" crop.

When Mommy and I plant our vegetable seeds, we make a straight row by tying a string between two sticks spread far apart in the ground.

I'm careful not to plant the seeds too close together so the poor plants won't grow on top of each other.

Another thing I love about the spring—besides picking daffodils and planting my vegetable garden—is that it's the best time to take long walks in the woods.

The swampy place is where the skunk cabbage grows. Although it's called cabbage, you can't eat it, and if you fold its leaves, guess what animal it smells like?

Jack-in-the-pulpits are wildflowers that grow from bulbs. The little "spike" looks just like a preacher in a pulpit. When I touch a plant, I'm always very gentle.

But there's one plant I NEVER touch, and that's poison ivy! It's a vine and easy to recognize. It has clusters of three shiny leaves that are green in spring and summer, and red in the fall.

When Mommy and I don't know the name of a plant, we look it up in our books about wildflowers. We don't *ever* pick anything in the woods. There are lots of wildflowers that don't exist anymore because people picked them.

The other way I learn about native plants and trees is by going to The New York Botanical Garden. Whenever I go, I invite Lily because it's one of our favorite outings. We play hide-and-seek in the American redbuds.

Mommy loves the dogwoods.

Juliet Alsop is the curator of the Native Plant Collection. If I go in the late spring, she shows me the yellow lady's slippers. They're very rare.

It's important never to pick lady's slippers. If this flower isn't allowed to make more seeds, there won't be more plants the next year.

During the early summer my seedlings start to sprout. From then on, it's just watering and weeding, weeding and watering.

I always save part of the garden for flowers, especially for cosmos, which are pink, white, magenta, and purple. Mommy and I pick them together.

We leave most of the marigolds where they are to scare off the bugs. But they're so pretty that I can't resist picking a few.

We always have enough corn on the cob to feed a small army. When the corn silk starts to turn brown, the corn is ready to pick.

By the end of the summer the real fun begins. Now I can EAT! Looking for tomatoes is like an Easter egg hunt.

When I pick the lettuce, I take the leaves from the outside of the plant so I'll keep getting more.

I planted some basil near the tomatoes and lettuce, so I have a complete salad in one spot.

September is sunflower month! They're bigger than I am.

Mommy and I strip the petals. Then we tie string around them and hang them up to dry. We hang them inside so the squirrels won't eat them.

In the winter, when the snow is on the ground, there's no food for the birds. We give them a special treat of our sunflower seeds, which they love. We put the seeds in a bird feeder outside our kitchen window and watch them feast.

September is also when we have our big garden picnic. Daddy helps me dig up the potatoes.

I love seeing all the different vegetables and flowers in one basket. Nature is really amazing.

This year I invited Lily to join us. We raced to see who could shuck the most corn. It was a tie.

Everything at our picnic came from the garden—corn, tomatoes, lettuce, herbs, potatoes—even the flowers on the table.

Lily was nervous that her loose tooth would fall out when she ate her corn on the cob. It didn't.

Nothing tastes better than food you've grown yourself.

During the winter I have a windowsill garden. I grow things from seeds, like grapefruit and avocado trees.

But mostly I'm waiting for spring. Gardeners are all the same that way!